Cambridge English

Starter Level

Series editor: Philip Prowse

Arman's Journey

Philip Prowse

CAMBRIDGE UNIVERSITY PRESS
Cambridge, New York, Melbourne, Madrid, Cape Town,
Singapore, São Paulo, Delhi, Tokyo, Mexico City

Cambridge University Press
The Edinburgh Building, Cambridge CB2 8RU, UK

www.cambridge.org
Information on this title: www.cambridge.org/9780521184939

First published 2011

Philip Prowse has asserted his right to be identified as the Author of the Work in
accordance with the Copyright, Designs and Patents Act 1988.

Printed in China by Sheck Wah Tong Printing Press Limited
Typeset by Aptara Inc.
Illustrations by Paul Dickinson
Map artwork by Malcolm Barnes
Cover image: © Richard Bowden / Alamy

A catalogue record of this book is available from the British Library.

ISBN 978-0-521-18493-9 paperback
ISBN 978-0-521-18496-0 paperback plus audio CD

Contents

People in the story

Arman:
lives in a
small town.

Leyla:
is Arman's
mother.

Dani:
is Arman's friend.

Jacob:
lives in London.
He is Leyla's uncle.

Fred:
lives in England.
Arman works for him.

Rose:
is Fred's daughter.

Places in the story

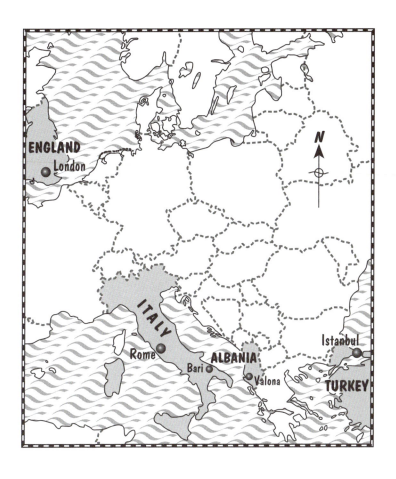

Chapter 1 *The soldiers*

'Arman!' shouts Leyla, my mother. 'Breakfast time!'

I'm seventeen and I live with my mother in a small town. My father is dead. I don't have any brothers or sisters, and we're not rich.

After breakfast I walk to school.

I see soldiers in front of a café.

There's fighting in the mountains near our town. Sometimes the soldiers come into town. They're looking for food and drink. And for young men to be soldiers with them.

Chapter 2 *Over the wall*

At twelve o'clock soldiers come to my school.

'Everyone out!' a tall soldier shouts.

'How old are you?' the soldier asks us all.

'Fourteen,' a short boy answers.

'You can go back to your room,' the soldier says. 'And you?' he asks me.

'Seventeen,' I answer.

'Over there,' the soldier says.

I go across to the other boys. We're all afraid.

The soldier smiles at us. I don't like his smile. 'Today's a very good day for you,' he says. 'You're coming with us. You're going to be soldiers.'

I don't want to be a soldier. I turn and run to the wall.

'Stop!' the soldier shouts and runs after me. But I'm very fast.

The wall is high, but I get over it. The soldier gets to the wall. But he doesn't come after me. I run quickly back to my house.

Chapter 3   *I don't want to go*

'Why are you here?' my mother asks.

I tell her about the soldiers.

'They're going to come to the school again and look for you,' she says. 'You can't live here any more. You must leave this country.'

'And go where?' I ask.

'Go to my uncle Jacob in England,' my mother answers.

'But I don't want to leave,' I say.

'Go in the morning or be a soldier. Like your father! And he's dead!' my mother shouts.

'But …' I start. 'England's far away. And I don't speak much English.'

'Jacob lives in London. He can find work for you. This is where he lives,' she answers. 'Tomorrow take a bus to the border. In the border town ask for Hamid. He knows how to get to England. But he wants lots of money. I have some money from your father. Here!'

'No,' I say.

'Take it,' she answers. 'Write to me when you're in England. Don't forget. You can give me money when you have work.'

The next day I say goodbye and take the bus. It's hot and the bus is slow. It stops at the border and the police get on. They don't say anything to me.

In the town I find Hamid. I give him a lot of my mother's money.

I go to the back of his truck. There's a young man there, called Dani. We're going to Turkey.

There are lots of melons in the truck. Hamid says, 'OK. Get under the melons.'

'Why?' I think. I find out when the truck stops. Police! But they don't look under the melons.

It's dirty in the truck and the roads are very bad.

Chapter 4 *Over the wall again*

We drive and drive for days. We're hot and tired.

'I never want to eat a melon again,' says Dani.

Then we stop near some mountains.

'OK,' Hamid says. 'Get out.'

'Now,' he says with a big smile. 'We're going for a little walk.'

The weather is very bad and everything is white with snow. We start to walk over the mountains. We're very cold and tired.

Then we hear a noise! Wolves! Six wolves are running up to us in the snow. Dani and I are afraid and don't know what to do. But Hamid does. He takes out a gun and five wolves run away. It's like a film!

We walk on over the mountains into Turkey. A truck is waiting for us. Dani and I sit with the driver.

'Goodbye!' Hamid shouts. 'Enjoy Istanbul!'

In Istanbul Dani and I get jobs, making jeans. We must have more money to get to England. It isn't easy work and I often think about my mother.

Dani and I sleep where we work. We're good friends now.

Dani knows about a man in Valona in Albania called Chichio. Chichio can get us to Italy for $2,000.

After three months we have the money and we leave for Albania by bus.

We find Chichio in Valona.

'There's a boat to Italy tonight,' he says. 'It takes ninety minutes.'

We give Chichio the money and leave at ten o'clock. There are twenty of us in the small fast boat – men, women, boys and girls. Everyone feels very cold.

We're near Italy when we hear another boat. It's the Italian border police. Chichio stops and takes out a gun. 'Now, get into the water or …'

We're all afraid. No-one opens their mouth. We look at the gun and do what Chichio says. Then he turns the boat and goes back to Albania.

The water is very cold and it's dark. The Italians can only find ten people. The others die in the cold water.

The police take us to Bari and put us in an old house with a high wall.

'What are you going to do?' I ask a policeman.

'You're going back to Albania,' he answers. 'Tomorrow.'

'What can we do?' I ask Dani.

'Wait,' he says.

We wait. Then there's only one policeman, and he's asleep. We run to the wall. It isn't easy, but we get over!

Chapter 5 *You must be Arman*

In the morning we take a train from Bari to Rome. But now we have no more money.

'Now,' Dani says, 'we must choose a truck which is going to England. Then we try and get in the back when the driver isn't looking.'

We find an English truck in Rome and get in. The driver doesn't know we're there. The truck leaves Rome. We have little food or water, and feel afraid and tired.

After thirty-six hours we get to England. The English border police don't find us. When the truck stops we get down. Now we're very happy!

Dani and I go to my mother's uncle, Jacob, in London.

'Ah! You must be Arman,' Jacob says. He has a kind face. 'I have a letter from your mother. But who's this?'

'It's my friend Dani,' I say.

We drink coffee and I tell Jacob about our journey.

'I must work,' I say. 'I must get money for my mother.'

Jacob smiles. 'It isn't easy, because you don't have work papers. There is work, but the money isn't good. Now you two must be tired after your long journey.'

'I'm going to write to my mother and tell her I'm here,' I say.

Chapter 6   *I'm going to call you Arm*

We live in Jacob's flat for three days. Then he says, 'Good! There are jobs for you!'

We take a bus out of the city. We're going to meet a man called Fred.

'What are your names?' Fred asks. He's a big man with red hair. I don't like him much.

'He's Dani,' I answer. 'And I'm Arman.'

'That's a funny name,' Fred says with a laugh. 'I'm going to call you Arm. Look, Arm. This is what you're going to do. See all these vegetables. You're going to put them on the truck. You start at six in the morning.'

We say thank you to Jacob and he goes back to London.

We sleep in a room with three young men. They're from other countries too, and don't speak much English.

At six in the morning, Fred takes us to work in a small bus. We work for six hours and stop for lunch. Then we work again for six hours. In the evening we cook food in our little kitchen.

The work isn't easy, but it's a job.

After a month, Fred gives me my money. It isn't very much.

'Sorry, Fred,' I start. 'About my money …'

'Listen, Arm!' Fred gets angry. 'You get a bed and food every day. I must have money for that.'

I don't say anything. I hate Fred. But my next letter to my mother has some money in it. Not a lot of money, but I'm helping my mother.

Chapter 7 *Rose*

Time goes by, and now I'm eighteen. The letters to my mother always have money in them.

Then, one morning, the bus has a new driver. She has long red hair and a beautiful smile.

'Hi,' she says. 'What's your name?'

When I tell her she says, 'Oh, my dad calls you Arm!'

'Is Fred your father?' I ask.

'Yes,' she answers. 'And I'm Rose.'

'That's a beautiful name,' I say.

Rose drives the bus every day. She asks me lots of questions about my country.

'How interesting!' she says. 'Living there can't be easy.'

In my next letter to my mother I write:

I have a new friend. Her name's Rose. She's the daughter of the man we work for. Some evenings she comes and teaches us English. I like her very much.

Rose and I often go for walks after the English lessons. She tells me about herself. She's helping her father this year. Then she's going to be a teacher.

One day I buy flowers for her.

'Roses for Rose.' I smile.

Rose laughs. 'Thank you very much, Arman,' she says. She never calls me Arm.

Rose takes my hand. 'I feel very happy,' she says.

'Me too,' I answer.

And then she kisses me. I close my eyes.

She smiles and says, 'It's late. I must go now. My father's waiting for me.'

I say goodbye to Rose. I think I'm a little in love with her. I don't know that someone's watching us – her father.

Chapter 8 *You can't make me*

The next evening, Rose looks sad.

'Is something wrong?' I ask. 'Why aren't you smiling? You always smile.'

Rose looks at me and says, 'I'm sorry, but the English lessons must finish.'

'Why?' I ask.

'It's my father,' Rose says. 'He knows about us. He doesn't want us to be friends.'

I take Rose in my arms.

'What are you doing, Arm?' someone shouts. It's Fred. 'Get away from my daughter!'

Rose looks at her father. 'I'm twenty-one,' she says. 'You can't tell me what to do.'

'Come with me!' Fred shouts.

'You can't make me,' answers Rose.

'Oh, yes I can!' Fred shouts again. He takes Rose away.

That night I don't sleep at all.

In the morning Fred is driving the bus.

'Arm!' Fred shouts when he sees me. His face is angry. 'You're going to work in the house today. It's dirty. Do you understand?'

'Yes,' I say and look at Dani. Dani looks away.

'Goodbye, Arm,' Fred says and takes out his phone. He gives me a cold smile. Then he speaks fast into the phone. I hear him say, 'Hello, please …' Or is he saying, 'Hello, police …'?

Chapter 9 *Police*

Fred drives off and I start work in the house.

After an hour I hear a car. I look out of the window and see a police car.

'What's your name?' the police ask at the door. 'Where are your work papers?'

I don't say anything.

'You must come with us,' the police say.

The police take me away. I just have a few things with me: my shirt and trousers, my phone and some money.

The next day I get a text.

I answer.

Hi Rose. I'm OK. The police say I must go back to my country.
They say I can't be in England. Love Arman

Chapter 10   *I'm coming*

After some weeks, the police put me on a plane. It takes eight hours from England to my country.

I phone my mother and then get a bus.

'You're here!' My mother's waiting at the door. She's very happy. 'It's good to see you, Arman,' she says. 'And there aren't any soldiers in the mountains now. You can live here again.'

I'm happy to be there, but I'm thinking of Rose.

Then I get a text.

Hi Arman. Are you well? I'm not helping my father any more. I have a new job. I'm going to teach English in Turkey. Can I meet you there? Love Rose

I tell my mother. I tell her what I'm going to do. She's sad, but she says, 'You must do what you want.'

I text Rose.